Down on the Farm

PIGS

Hannah Ray

Crabtree Publishing Company

www.crabtreebooks.com

Published by Crabtree Publishing Company

Copyright © 2008

www.crabtreebooks.com

PMB16A
350 Fifth Ave., Suite 3308
New York, NY 10118

616 Welland Ave.
St. Catharines, Ontario
L2M 5V6

First published in hardcover in the U.S.A. in 2006
by QEB Publishing, Inc.

Cataloging-in-Publication data is available at the
Library of Congress.

ISBN 10: 0-7787-4055-2 paperback
ISBN 13: 978-0-7787-4055-1 paperback

Printed and bound in China

Written by Hannah Ray
Designed by Liz Wiffen
Consultant Sally Morgan
Editor Paul Manning
Picture Researcher Joanne Forrest Smith
Illustrated by Chris Davidson

Publisher Steve Evans
Editorial Director Jean Coppendale
Art Director Zeta Davies

Picture credits

Key: t = top, b = bottom, c = center,
l = left, r = right, FC = front cover

Alamy /Penny Boyd 7, /David Hoffman Photo
Library 5, /Holt Studios/Sarah Rowland 17T,
/Renee Morris 4, 11; **Corbis** /Claro Cortes IV
19, /Robert Dowling 16T, /Owen Franken 15B,
/Peter Worth 9; **FLPA** /Jurgen & Christine
Sohns 16B; **Getty Images** /Peter Cade 8B,
/Robert Daly 14, /Bob Elsdale 13, 22, /Bill
Ling 6, /Thorsten Milse FC, 1, 8T, /Antony
Nagelmann 10, /Ryan Pierse 18, /Robert Ross
17B, /Andy Sacks 12.

CONTENTS

Words in **bold** can be found in the Glossary on page 22.

Pigs on the farm

Do you know where ham and bacon come from? Or the pork sausages that you cook for breakfast? What about the **bristles** in your paintbrush? All these things come from pigs.

Farmers all over the world raise pigs. Pigs give us lots of different types of meat. They are found everywhere except Antarctica.

Pigs from nose to tail

A full-grown pig is about 32 inches (80 cm) tall at the shoulder and weighs about 200 lbs. (90 kg). That's the same weight as four and a half six-year-old children!

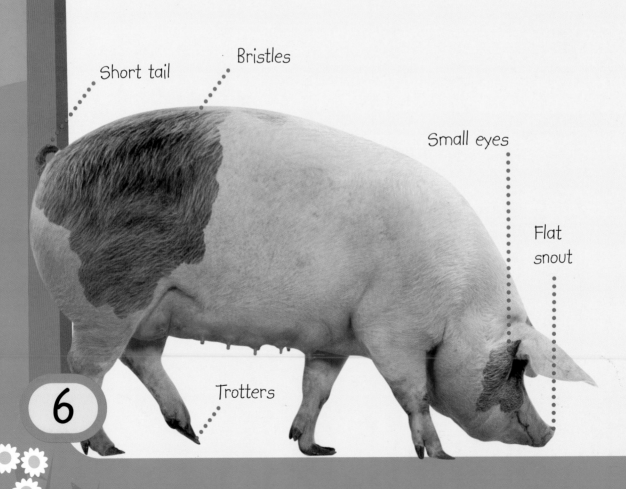

Short tail

Bristles

Small eyes

Flat snout

Trotters

In some countries, there are still wild pigs called boars. Some boars have **tusks**.

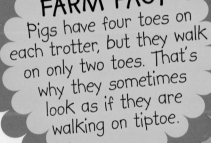

Height of six-year-old child

Height of pig

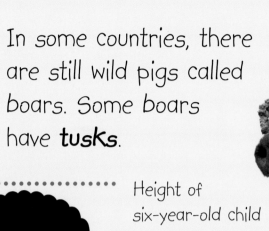

FARM FACT
Pigs have four toes on each trotter, but they walk on only two toes. That's why they sometimes look as if they are walking on tiptoe.

It's a pig's life...

A baby pig is called a piglet. Before a piglet is born, it grows inside its mother for 16 weeks. The mother pig, or sow, can give birth to about 18 piglets in one **litter**.

For the first few weeks, the piglets feed on their mother's milk.

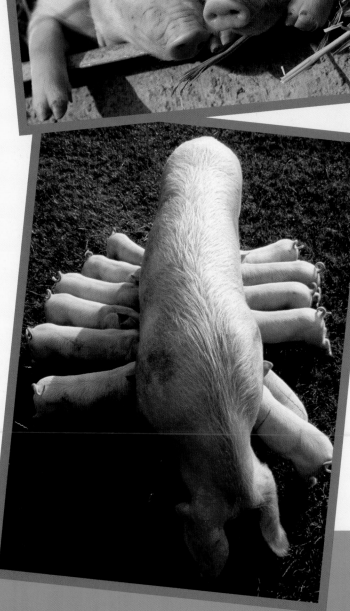

A mother pig feeding her babies

FARM FACT
The biggest pig in the world was called Big Bill. He weighed 2,252 pounds. That's the same as 14 full-grown men!

These Saddleback piglets are about 14 weeks old.

At two weeks old, the piglets start to eat other food, too, such as **grain**, plants, and vegetable scraps.

At seven months, a female pig is big enough to have babies of her own. Sows usually give birth to two litters every year.

On a farm, pigs can live for 10 to 15 years.

9

Big bad pig?

Many people think that pigs are smelly, dirty, and not very smart, but this is not true.

Pigs are very smart. In fact, they are more intelligent than dogs and cats.

FARM FACT
In hot weather, pigs use mud to protect themselves from the sun's rays. They can get sunburned, just like you!

Pigs do not roll in mud because they like being dirty. They do it to cool down because they cannot **sweat**.

Pigs keep their **nest** very clean. They go to the bathroom as far away as possible from where they sleep.

11

Piggy pals

Pigs are very friendly. They can use up to 20 different noises to speak to each other.

Newborn piglets will run to their mother when she calls them. When the piglets are only five to ten days old, their mother encourages them to leave the nest to meet other pigs.

Piglets are very playful animals.
They enjoy play-fighting and
throwing things
into the air, just
for fun!

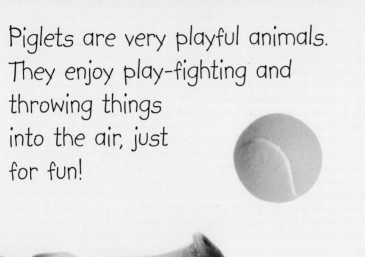

13

From pork to paintbrushes

Pigs are raised mainly for their meat, but they give us other things, too. Leather called pigskin is used to make gloves, wallets, purses, footballs, and belts.

Pigs give us sausages, bacon, ham, and pork.

In some countries, such as France, pigs are used to find rare wild **fungi** called truffles, which grow underground. The pigs use their amazing sense of smell to hunt out the truffles and dig them up with their snouts.

14

FARM FACT
The bristles that grow on a pig's skin are used to make special paintbrushes, called hogshair brushes.

A pig sniffing for truffles.

Pigs around the world

MIDDLE WHITE

These funny-faced pigs are from Yorkshire, England. They are very good-natured and talkative.

SWABIAN HALL SWINE

These pigs come from Germany and they are famous for their meat. They can be recognized by their black heads and black tails.

GLOUCESTER OLD SPOT

These large pigs are an old English breed. They were once called "**orchard pigs**" because they ate the apples that fell to the ground in apple orchards.

RED RIVER HOG

These unusual wild pigs live in western and central Africa. They rest during the day and are active at night.

Piggy customs

FRANCE

Every August in a town in the south of France, the people celebrate everything piggy. There is a prize for the best pig costume, a piglet race and even a pig **imitation** contest!

Piglet racing in the south of France.

PHILIPPINES

In June every year, roasted pigs are carried through towns in the Philippines and are eaten at a big party. The roasted pigs are called "lechons."

CHINA

In China, each year is named after one of twelve animals. People born in the Chinese Year of the Pig always tell the truth and are good friends. They try their best at everything.

FARM FACT

Pigs can swim! In fact, a pig called Priscilla is even said to have saved a small boy from drowning!

19

Make a piggy bank

To make this fun piggy bank, you will need lots of strips of newspaper, some wallpaper paste, a balloon, an egg carton, a pipe cleaner, some masking tape, a marker, and lots of pink paint.

1 Blow up the balloon. Stick on three or four complete layers of newspaper strips, using lots of wallpaper paste.

2 Let the layers dry out overnight. Then pop the balloon and remove it. You now have your piggy body.

20

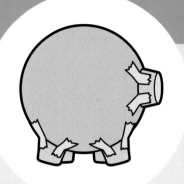

3 With masking tape, stick on four egg-carton legs, an egg-carton snout, and two cardboard flaps for the ears.

4 Bend the pipe cleaner into a curly tail and stick it on with masking tape.

5 Paint your pig and let it dry. Then draw on eyes and a big smile.

6 Ask a grownup to cut a slot in the top of your pig, so that you can put money into your piggy bank.

Glossary and Index

bristle thick hair that grows on a pig's skin, used to make paintbrushes and hairbrushes

fungi mushrooms, toadstools, and truffles that grow wild in woods and fields

grain food from plants such as wheat, barley, or corn

imitation copying, or pretending to be, something or someone

litter a number of baby pigs that are all born at one time

nest an area where a pig sleeps, often a pile of straw

orchard a field where fruit trees grow

sweat when our skin becomes damp to help us cool down

tusk long, pointed tooth on a boar or elephant

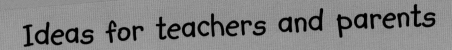

Ideas for teachers and parents

- Make a pig poster. Take a large sheet of paper and draw the outline of a pig. Look through comic books, magazines, and newspapers and cut out anything pig-related. Look out for scraps of pink material, buttons, or ribbons. Collect your odds and ends and use them to fill in the pig outline.

- Research different breeds of pigs and make fact sheets comparing the children's favorite breeds.

- Visit a county fair or children's farm so the children can see real pigs.

- Help the children make a list of all the stories they know that feature pigs, for example, The Three Little Pigs.

- Find poems about pigs and help the children make up a funny pig poem of their own. Use lots of words beginning with the letter "p." Try writing your poem in a pig shape.

- Have fun making piggy noises with the children. Who can snort the loudest?

- Make a simple word search puzzle for the children using pig-related vocabulary from this book.

- Make a thumbprint pig picture. Help the children to draw a barnyard scene on a large sheet of paper and make thumbprints around the barnyard using pink fingerpaints. When the pink paint is dry, use a felt-tip marker to add legs, a curly tail, a snout, eyes, and a big smile to each "pig."

- Make a pig mask out of a paper plate. Paint the plate pink and cut out eyeholes. Cut out a pair of floppy ears from pink felt and stick them to the mask. Add an egg-carton nose and draw on a piggy smile. Add holes to each side of the mask and tie on a piece of elastic so the mask can be worn.

24